The World of the Persians

The World of the Persians

Texts by **J.-A. de Gobineau**

John Gifford
London

Contents:

© Editions Minerva S.A., Genève, 1971.

A typical landscape in the hearth of Iran, near Persepolis.

From the Caspian Sea to the Indian Ocean and from the Mountains of Assyria to those of India: a country whose average height above sea level is over three thousand feet and whose area is three times as big as that of France; two-thirds desert, it is true, but rich in its watered areas — that is Iran, long known as Persia.

1 - Early times; primitive life.

In very remote times the white race began to settle into its first home in the heights of Asia. It slowly spread into the west and south-west of the continent. One by one, its growing tribes separated. Some of them, having penetrated into Europe, were to become the Celts, the Thracians, the Latins, the Hellenes and the Slavs. At the same time, other no less important branches of the original stock, moving southwards, took with them a flourishing population, of which one group long remained connected with their motherland: the Scythians. Another, having separated from them, turned eastwards and became the progenitors of the Hindus: then a third, splitting off much later from the Scythians and the future votaries of Brahma, and putting behind them the springs of the Indus, reached the lands of Central Asia, to give birth to the peoples whom the Greeks and Romans called the Persians, but who still use the name Iranian for themselves.

The Greeks, who gave us the term "Persian" for the Iranian nations, used this word because at the time when they were confronting the dominating race of Western Asia the province of "Perside" ("Pars" in the indigenous language) was the ruling nation of the empire and because the chief posts in government and senior military appointments were usually conferred on members of that nation. The ruling family itself, if not originating in the country, was at least domiciled there, so that the name "Persian", applied to members of the ruling class under Cyrus's régime, understandably came to be used for the whole race. Mohammedan chronicles carry evidence of this old style, and it is not uncommon to find the term "Parsy", or in Arab transcription "Farsy" for the more usual and correct "Irany". This name itself is nothing other than "Ayrian" or "Aryan", which was the name common to all the white races at their origin.

The migrants moved onwards into the lands they discovered along with their women, children, dogs and cattle. They were seeking a suitable place for agriculture, a place with fresh running water, which was capable of being defended against attackers. It appears in fact that the sites of their first settlements were chosen to serve as fortresses.

First, they would mark out a square enclosure the length of a "meydan" the distance a horse set off on the gallop will continue until it stops of its own accord. In the centre was lit the sacred fire, the palladium of that place. Here were hired domestic servants. It was scrupulously tended day and night, never being allowed to go out. Every three days the flame was carried to the communal living-place, where its purity was re-born.

This idea of the never-dying fire is certainly one of the oldest of the national religions of the original white race, in view of the fact that the branch which settled in Italy introduced the Vesta cult there. An equally obvious example is the myth of Prometheus, revered as a demi-god and a person of divine intervention, the "pra-mantha", accredited with the power of producing fire at will.

7

Opposite and above, the remains of a ziggurat in Susiana. Ziggurats, built of clay or burnt brick, were towers serving religious purposes.

At the side of the flame they used to hollow out a pool whose dimensions bore a relationship to the size of the population. When the pool had been filled it was continually guarded to ensure that the water was always pure, mainly for religious reasons but also because the water was used for domestic purposes.

When the fire and the pool were established they then set about building their houses. These were of one or two storeys, built in pillars, and around them extended courtyards and lodges varying in size according to the wealth of the owner.

Next to the first enclosure, to which a single gate set into a high watchtower gave access, they set out another one of identical size. This was used as a place of safety for the animals during the night, in the winter when snow made it impossible for them to wander about, or when enemies were attacking. Around this enclosure, dogs prowled incessantly, and no doubt it was because of their services in this way that these animals came to earn the respect, even the love that was accorded them.

In the description of Iranian society set out in the Vendidad, dogs are named immediately after free men. To strike them was nothing less than a crime. To feed them too much rich or hot food brought serious punishment. To neglect to take especial care of bitches about to give birth rendered the guilty party liable to public shame and retribution. Lack of attention for the pups was equivalent to neglecting Iranian children. In no other society has the dog been such a friend, such a companion, almost the equal of man, so that even today, from ancestral memory of the watch they kept day and night over the homes of their progenitors, they say in Persia that a "dyw" (demon) cannot tolerate their look and must flee before it.

The Arians were essentially an agricultural people. According to their totally naturalistic ideas the whole world lived, felt and understood their life; and the whole world, earth and sky, was organized for the benefit of mankind, which was consequently obliged to be diligent to care for and continue the work of creation.

"When does the earth rejoice?" they used to say.

9

"When a pure man comes near who is prepared to offer a sacrifice."

"And then?"

"When a pure man builds himself a home, provides it with fire, and cattle, and brings to it a wife and children; and when in this home grow with decency, dogs and forage and everything that belongs to the good life."

"And then?"

"When the cultivation of the earth brings forth harvests, plants and fruitful trees; and when skilfully directed waters fertilise the lands and cause the marshes to dry up."

Even if the style of life of the original inhabitants did not allow any luxury, it meant certain well-being as a result of hard work, as well as a kind of military panache which appealed to the imaginations of a people closely aware of the splendours of creation and desirous of imitating its shapes and colours. The Vendidad mentions two kinds of dress, those made out of the skins of animals, and those made from woven materials of hair and wool. These clothes were made at home, the women of the house-hold doing most of the work. Apart from this we have no reason for thinking that industry as such, in our sense of the word, existed at all amongst the Aryans. Their social system knew nothing comparable, and in fact their whole set of ideas militated against it. Being full of deep veneration for all the diverse manifestations of Nature, which they conceived as being capable of living, feeling and thinking, and of suffering as well as being joyous, the Aryans disapproved of the use and application of fire in a great number of circumstances. Therefore many trades were debarred from the outset. They feared that the sanctity of fire, the purity of water, the inviolability of stone would be destroyed by incorrect use, so this was not permitted except within very narrow limits. All the same, this dogma was eased in some matters: in mining, for example, which had been authorized from very early times. The Scythians, the Indians, as well as the men of Iran, learned early the use of gold and iron.

The Aryans, clothed in tunics of wool or skins, would sit before the sacred hearths of their homes. They would eat the flesh of their herds and particularly products of milk, which were especially recommended in the holy texts as being a pure food. Amongst these, those deriving from mare's milk were most approved of by religion.

Their houses and fortresses were built of blocks of stone set on one another according to their natural size and shape. These blocks could not be cut because this would have sullied the purity of stone and been against the law. This was a point of dogma that the Arian was obliged to follow from his respect for Nature.

For hunting, and no doubt in war as well, the Arians used what is called in America the "lasso", a long rope with weights attached and which they used to call the

10

Part of a horse's bit, and a complete bit, in bronze. Period 900 B.C.

13

"çnavara". Across their shoulders they wore the yoke, which was incorporated by the ancient Greeks into their myth of Hercules. Their copper cuirasses were decorated with figures of tigers and other beasts of prey.

They certainly possessed horses, since they used to consume mares' milk. Bulls and cows were also used, not only as beasts of burden but as mounts. The great warriors of early times are always depicted riding on bulls.

One of the most central and significant features of the mythology of the white races was what the Greeks, for example, called "ambrosia", the drink of the gods. Amongst the Hindus it was "amrita", which seems to be another form of the same word. To the Scandinavians it was "the heavenly beer of the gods", who brewed it themselves with special care. The Iranian Aryans knew it as "homa", which was also the word used by the Indian Aryans.

Homa is a plant which grows in present-day Turkestan, once Sogdian, and in places further north, the first home of the Aryans. It is also found on the mountain slopes of Kerman. The botanical name is "sarcostema viminalis". When the stalks or ground-up shoots are mixed with curdled milk, barley meal or a cereal known to the Hindus as "nivara" or "trinadhanya", which might have been wild rice, and the resulting liquor left to ferment, a strong and intoxicating brew is produced which is considered

14

Statuette of a man, in stone and gold. 3,000 B.C. (Foraughi Museum, Teheran). The bronze on the right was used to decorate a chariot.

healthy, nutritious and capable of providing strength as well as prolonging life. For this reason the gods of the Hindu pantheon rejoiced in its use.

It is easy to understand how the Hellene Aryans considered ambrosia as much a food, as we see from Homer, as a drink; since it was derived from plants and grain it would naturally be fit to serve as nourishment.

The Iranians were religious to an extreme degree. The heart of their society and the mainspring of all their actions was unceasing contact with what we would call the supernatural, but which for them was the real world in which they lived. To their minds nothing was more mysterious and inexplicable than their own existence, so that it was no more difficult to explain the invisible and incessant actions of the gods than to account for how and why they themselves found themselves on the earth. As they considered they belonged to a decidedly superior order of beings, they found it quite acceptable that there should be a more superior order again, where their ancestors dwelled, and to which they might aspire in their turn.

They erected no temples. They constructed no material representations of the objects of their veneration. Sacrifices, hymns and prayers sufficed. All Nature was a boundless and illimitable object of respect. The whole Creation was made for them: to serve and benefit them in every way, and to receive their eulogies.

Ornament from a bridle of very early date. Right, two aspects of eternal Iran.

Head of a breast-pin dating from 1,000 B.C., and a figurine of a woman from the same period. (Herramaneck Museum, New York.)

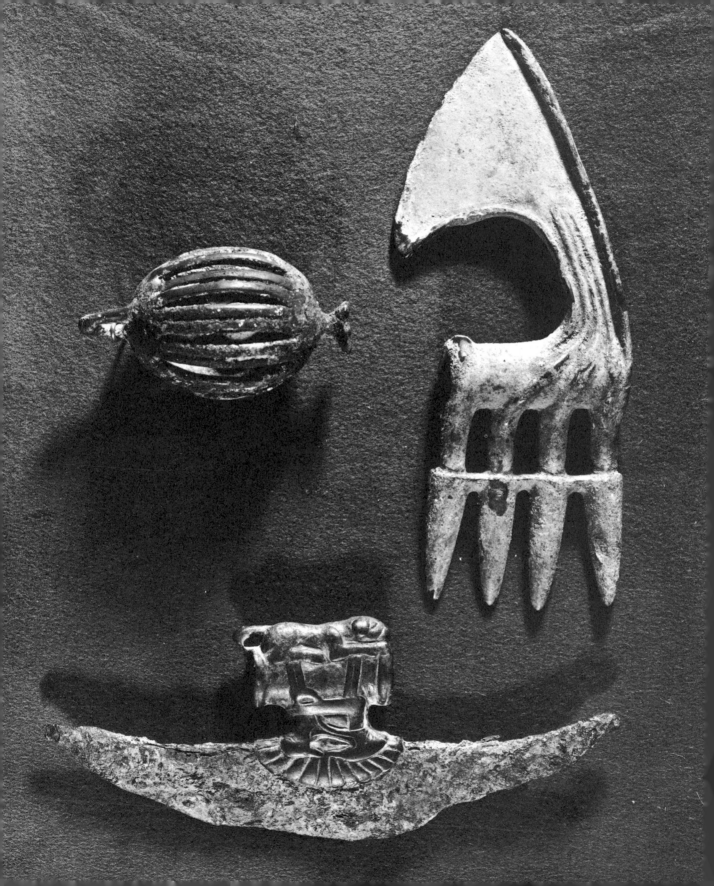

*Two axes and a bowl, bronze. 900 B.C.
(Louvre, Paris).*

In those times no one believed that man could acquire such sublime knowledge by his own efforts. Neither could God reveal his truth without an intermediary. There had already been two initiations. The first came by means of the bird Karshipta, lost in the depths of time. The second had a man as propagator, a *voyant* named by the Vendidad as Ourvatat-Naro.

Even though the Arians had no temples or tangible images of divinity, the domestic altar or perhaps (and probably) the communal altar erected by a group of worshippers served the same purpose. The sacrifice became more important, and by the same token the accompanying rites and ceremonies became more mystical because they were not shared with the adoration of the faithful. The central feature of the cult was undoubtedly the sacrifice. This was the most prestigious act man could perform for the gods, and the one which the gods esteemed most highly. In accordance with this tradition many religions today employ the symbolism of sacrifice as the most sublime expression of their faith.

In the very first stages of the Aryan peoples' existence, while they were still uninfluenced by alien ideas, we know that they used to sacrifice living victims on their altars. The whole white race is aware that this is one of their most seated traditions.

Human sacrifices were performed on five especial occasions. The first was when any edifice was to be constructed, in order to to ensure that it would last. This idea is met in Roman traditions as well as in those of the Slavs and Germans. The victim's head was separated from the trunk, which was thrown into the water to be used for making the bricks. The head itself was buried in the foundations.

The second was on the occasion of a regal consecration. The third was the "Acvamedha", or "horse sacrifice": the devout victim was held under water until he drowned, when the horse's blood was poured over his head.

The fourth occasion was at the winter solstice, but no record of these ceremonies has come down to us, and no race-memories seem to remain. For the fifth, however, we know that they used to select a Brahmin as victim, who was well paid and given every luxury for a whole year (except that total celibacy was required). When the appointed time came he was dressed in a rich red robe woven from the threads of the plant called "kouca", and choked to death.

Herodotus recounts how when Xerxes came to the river Struma and found nine roads finishing there he buried alive nine boys and nine girls belonging to the country, in accordance with Persian custom, the historian adds. In this connection he recalls how Xerxes' wife, Amestris, buried alive fourteen children as a sop to the gods in her old age.

The Iranians also sacrificed horses, as did the Indians, the Scythians, the Germans

21

and the Franks. Of lesser importance was the sacrifice of sheep and goats.

Legend puts at the head of royal genealogy a figure by the name of Keyoumers. With an exactitude for which we must be grateful it adds that this was not his real name, which remains unknown, but was assumed by him on taking up his role as monarch.

In fact, Keyoumers is not a name at all, properly speaking. It is actually a title, meaning nothing more than "king of the country", or perhaps "king of men", depending on how one reads the Persian spelling. The word "Key" to describe the monarch is common to the original Aryan languages, and seems to be cognate with a root meaning " to give birth", or "create". So words like "Key", "Kava", "Kau", "Kung", "Konungr", "Konig", "King", originally meant the head of the family, with his wife, sons and daughters, then with his slaves, protégés, tenants, mercenaries, and finally subjects and conquered peoples.

The population was divided into families, which were grouped into tribes; these were formed into associations which in their turn made up the social order of a country. This way of organizing a nation is seen with extreme clarity amongst the original Greeks; it is still seen in Israel, and of course the present-day German system shows evidence of it. It is natural to the race. Each subdivision has its own chief or head: that of the family, then the tribe, the tribal association and so on, and finally the sovereign himself, who is nothing more than the head of the whole hierarchy, which he can do nothing to change and which has its own existence independently of the regal will, which is itself dependent on the acceptance of those beneath him. He confers with powerful men; without them he can achieve nothing except by the use of senseless and wasteful violence.

In the beginnings two forms of authority can be deduced. First of all the magistrate, or king, ruling over the Aryans with the limited powers granted him by the chiefs; then the general, the overlord of the tribes necessitated by the organization of common defence. Out of this system was to flow the struggle between despotism and libertarianism, a struggle which in many places was to finish in victory for despotism.

As the Aryans believed that the gods were constantly preoccupied with their affairs they settled legal cases by the proof of boiling water and similar methods. These were a suitable way of allowing the powerful keepers of the truth to show what the truth was. Indians, Hellenes, Hebrews and the Franks of the Middle Ages all used and approved such methods. To swear on oath was profanation and indignity for a man of noble race, whose word should suffice. To conclude an agreement, a handshake was as good as a bond. To refuse a suppliant was inadmissible. It was a crime to make advances to a pregnant woman, or to harm her in any way, and to abandon a girl whom one had seduced rendered one liable to serious penalties. If

she destroyed the child of the union through fear of shame, she would be severely punished. At the same time it was considered healthy and respectable for close relatives to marry, and so we hear of the union of brothers and sisters, which so astonished the Greeks at the time of Herodotus.

There was an obligation on all Aryans to destroy dangerous animals and everything impure, especially reptiles, whose nests had to be destroyed and broods exterminated.

We have already seen that a dog's look could make demons flee. For this reason,

and because of the great esteem the Aryans had for their faithful family friends, dogs always accompanied funerals. The Greeks had forgotten the reason for this custom: they merely associated dogs with the world of the Shades. A dog guarded the lower regions, and a particular god, Hermes, had been given the task of conveying the souls of the departed to their final homes. Reasonably enough, scholars find in Hermes an association with the dog, the animal whose allotted task it was to protect the dead from evil spirits and at the same to play the leading part at funereal rites.

A time came when stones began to be hewn, when palaces, mansions, cities and fortresses began to be built on a far more elaborate scale than hitherto. The earth itself was ransacked in the search for minerals. Weapons of iron replaced the traditional wood and stone. Helmets, cuirasses, swords, lances, bronze-headed arrows were manufactured. To decorate these new inventions, as well as the thrones and chariots, the crowns and bracelets, the usefulness of precious stones was realized, and so the search for diamonds, emeralds, rubies, turquoises, cornalines and opals began.

Such flamboyancies would not have sat well on the simple clothes people had been contented with until then. So silk and wool were woven into cloth; it is interesting to note that there was no reference to cotton being used for this purpose. These materials, which were much suppler, richer and finer

Wall foundations of brick, with a frieze composed of circles. — Ornamentation on a goblet found in Susa: reversed swastikas. 1,000 to 2,000 B.C.

than those known before, were dyed in different colours and embroidered in a thousand different ways. They learned to design and cut them in styles to satisfy the most fastidious taste. They discovered the charm of perfume, using musk, amber, incense and aloe; these are mainly derived from scented woods such as sandal, which were originally quite scarce and sought-after. It was not long before a strong and passionate people, fond of material excess, discovered the use of wine, and this is how legend recounts it.

One day King Djem was sitting in his tent, watching his archers practising, when there appeared in the sky a great bird hardly able to fly because of a snake which had wrapped itself around its neck. This would be an intolerable sight to an Arian, since birds belonged to Good Creation while reptiles were the most frightful of the Bad. Djem ordered one of his archers to aim at the snake and kill it, and to take care not to harm the bird. The arrow delivered a mortal blow to the snake, which immediately released its prey and fell to the ground, while the bird flew off and disappeared over the horizon.

Not many moments passed before it reappeared and landed on the ground in front of Djem, and as if wishing to show its gratitude dropped some seeds from its beak at his feet.

These seeds, which were of a kind no one had seen before, were picked up and planted, and in a little time put forth a plant which

27

grew and flourished in its season, producing beautiful fruit in great bunches. It was the vine.

The king noticed that the delicate skin of the lovely fruit enclosed a liquid content which would be easy to separate from the pips; so he set his servants to work to do this, and enclosed the resulting juice in a jar. After a few days the king decided to taste it, no doubt assuming it would be something like mead or similar drinks. However, he was repelled by such a strange, bitter taste that he thought it must be poisonous and kept it on one side with the thought — or so the oriental narrator candidly opines — that it might one day be useful in affairs of state.

It so happened however that Djem had a very beautiful and dearly loved girl slave. One day when he was out hunting she was taken ill with violent pains in the head so that she was unable to have a moment's rest. Nothing that others could do could bring her solace. At last, driven mad and in despair, the poor girl decided to kill herself and remembered the poison the king had put aside. She opened the jar and began to drink. She drank so much that she fell asleep, and when she awoke she found that she was perfectly well again.

When Djem returned, she told him what had happened. As a result the king changed his opinion on the nature of the beverage whose recipe he had discovered; instead of using it for devious purposes of state he

used it as a medecine, with such success in so many cases that wine came to be known to the old Persians as "Darou-e-Shah", meaning "the king's medecine".

The great bird which was attacked by the impure snake and saved by an Aryan's arrow and which in gratitude brought to mankind blessings it had not hitherto enjoyed must surely have been the legendary Karshipta.

The Vendidad describes medical science in those days as being composed of three equally important divisions, or what we would nowadays call specialities. One dealt in treatment by propitiatory methods; another by the application of what we might call herbal remedies, either externally or internally, while the thrid specialized in surgery. It was the first method, that of "manthra-spenta", which in the opinion of the Vendidad was the most commendable. I do not think we should confuse this with the use of magical formulas which became so widespread later on. Rather it was a case of simple supplication to the gods to appeal for their help.

The rules of the Avesta on the subject of medicine give us an insight into the economic affairs of the early Iranians which is illuminating. The holy book does not disdain to set out the fees due to practitioners of the art.

An Athrava, a priest who had been cured, would repay his benefactor with a pious benediction. This counted for much, as people had such enormous confidence in the power of words of this sort. The chief of a

household, the head of a family, would give a small beast of burden. The head of a village would pay by means of an animal of moderate size, but a powerful lord would have to provide a draught beast of major size. From a prince the doctor would have to receive four beef cattle. A housewife would give a donkey, the wife of a village head, a mare; a princess would give a camel, and so on. It seems clear from all this that if there was no cure there was no fee. We also see in practice the fundamental principle on which Asiatics still base their ideas of value, which is not that there is any intrinsic price to be set on goods or services, but that everything depends on the abilty of the purchaser to pay. So the poor buy cheaply what the rich have to pay dearly for.

This plant peculiar to Iran is a kind of broom.
It has white flowers, called "chapour".

A royal head. Date 600 B.C.

The Medes, settled in the North of Iran, formed for a long time the most powerful people in Asia Minor. Their country was ravaged several times by the Scythians who came from the plains between the Danube and the Don and were formidable horse-men: chronicles record Scythian armies of 800,000 men, which however were finally beaten. The priests of the Medes were the Magi who, dressed in voluminous white robes, each wearing a tiara and carrying a branch, offered sacrifices whilst chanting magic formulas, and predicted the future from observations of the stars.

The ruler of Persia and Susiana was a vassal of the Mede empire. Cyrus was to rise up against this state of affairs: he managed to beat the Medish troops and thus set about building a vast State.

2 - Cyrus. The conquest of Babylon. The Jews.

The fame of the great Cyrus has traversed the centuries, yet actual details of the man himself are few. He can be said without fear of contradiction to rank amongst the five or six greatest leaders of humanity; but if we want to know what he was really like, or what he really did, the answers remain obscure. Many legends and self-contradictory traditional stories are available to us, not to mention Xenophon's tedious account and a few anecdotes to be found in the Greek authors; but leaving these aside, the only historical evidence seems to be of a few modest conquests, certainly not enough to justify such fame.

Be that as it may, there is no doubt that in Asian annals Cyrus's reign marked the beginning of a new epoch.

Herodotus recounts how Astyages, king of Media, dreamed one night that his daughter Mandane urinated so copiously that his capital city of Ecbatana and the whole of Asia were completely flooded. When he consulted the Magis they frightened him so much that he dared not give his daughter in marriage to a Mede, fearing that his son-in-law would prove a dangerous competitor. So he married her to a Persian, Cambyses, a courteous and sweet-tempered man of good family, but quite definitely inferior to any Mede of even moderate status, according to Astyages' way of thinking. The Persians were in fact merely vassals of the Median empire, being governed only by nominees.

At the end of the first year of Cambyses' marriage to Mandane, Astyages had another dream. This time he dreamed that a vine-tree grew from his daughter's breast that covered the whole of Asia. The interpretation placed on this latest vision terrified him even more than the first: he caused Mandane, who was now pregnant, to come before him and kept her more or less prisoner. When her child was born he took it away from her and sent it to her kinsman Harpagus with orders to kill it, whereupon he felt more secure.

But Harpagus feared the king might change his mind, or that there might be difficulties when the question of succession inevitably arose and he would be confronted with an angry Mandane, a disappointed mother; so he disobeyed the order and entrusted the infant to one of Astyages' cow-herds, by the name of Mithradates. This man's wife's name was Spaco, which according to Herodotus means "bitch" in the Median language. The two of them took the child with them into the pastures to the north of Ecbatana, towards Euxin. They had orders to expose him on the mountain, at the foot of the woods, so that the wild beasts would eat him up. As chance had it, however, Spaco had just given birth to a still-born child, and they decided to leave

her dead infant on the mountain and bring up Mandane's son as their own.

Ten years later the young Cyrus, who at that time had a different name given to him by his foster parents, became recognized by the truly regal disdain with which he treated the son of a Median lord when playing kings and queens with other children of his own age. Astyages quickly discovered the truth and punished Harpagus's treachery by making him eat his own child. So assuaged, he made peace with himself and allowed Cyrus to live, since the Magis as-sured him that by asserting his regality Cyrus had fulfilled the oracle's predictions and that there were no grounds for thinking that he would overthrow his grandfather. From that time on, nothing stood in the way of Cyrus assuming his true princely status, which is what indeed happened; on the orders of his grandfather he went amongst the Persians to find his father Cambyses and his mother Mandane, and everyone believed that he had been brought up by a bitch, because his foster-mother's name was Spaco. So Hero-dotus relates.

*A Mede and a Persian
conversing.*

At the tip of Asia, opposite Greece, lay the rich kingdom of Lydia near which the Greeks had founded cities as famous as Smyrna, Ephesus and Miletus. This country has the distinction of being the first in the world to produce coinage. Its king was the celebrated Cresus who became so worried at the increase in Cyrus's power that he challenged it. The results were unfortunate: Persia annexed Lydia. Emboldened by this success Cyrus decided to attack the king of Babylon whose unpopularity he had just heard of.

Remains of a great bas-relief, in black stone, at Pasagardes, Cyrus's capital.

Remains of a bas-relief from the entrance to Cyrus's palace in Pasagardes: a four-winged figure clad in the Egyptian style. Right, Cyrus's tomb, erected in his palace gardens.

Remains of Cyrus's palace, and wall-joints.

Confluence of the Tigris and Euphrates, near Babylon, and the delta of the two rivers.

Babylon in its final days conformed to all the conditions necessary for a monarchy to collapse in the face of the slightest subversive force. It was a splendid, wealthy city which had benefited as much as Sardis by the fall of famous Niniveh. Placed as it was in the middle of lush plains rich in grain and palms, it gathered within its walls traders from every nation certain of making handsome profits from dealing in the exotic range of goods set out in its bazaars. Neither famine nor drought could halt or arrest its growing wealth, since it was not dependent on the uncertain spring or autumn rains that India is subject to. The two great rivers, the Tigris and the Euphrates, fertilized its plains and provided it with a totally reliable source of water; in addition there was an elaborate canal system using the secondary rivers and streams debouching from the Kurdistan hills, which could be controlled at will, so that even under the burning southern sun the land was perpetually fresh and well-watered to produce the richest and lushest vegetation.

With all its natural advantages and abundance of raw materials a country like this is bound to create great wealth. Egypt is the classic example, and so was Babylon as long as the population was maintained. Thanks to its agriculture, all manner of people flocked there: the Phoenicians, who had opened up Corsica, Sardinia, Spain and the Scilly Isles; the Egyptians bringing produce from their own country and from Ammon; the Ethiopians bearing gold and ivory from

Africa; the Arabs, the perfume-sellers; and the Indians, whose merchandise of precious materials showed a quality of workmanship which was a wonder and delight in those far-off days. All these strangers, with their differing faces, colouring, height and gait, jostled incessantly through the streets of the great city, displaying their motley cloaks, exotic national head-dress, the felt hats of the Assyrians, carrying walking-sticks made of rare woods decorated with artistically carved symbols such as a bird or a flower.

Babylon was not only the great commercial centre of the world, the recognized market-place for trade on a large scale; nor was it only the great meeting-place for travellers, who used it to exchange news and ideas about each other's national customs and laws, no doubt astonishing each other in the process: it had an even greater claim to fame as the established centre of the most complete and advanced science hitherto known. Its priests and doctors in their colleges had evolved a far-reaching intellectual system which embraced all aspects of nature, both material and metaphysical.

The good and the bad, the splendours and the miseries were piled up together in this enormous city, whose equally enormous population so impressed the imagination of people at the time that we wonder whether in attempting to describe it they may have been even more prone to exaggeration than usual.

A wall three hundred feet high and

seventy-five wide, a veritable mountain it might be said, enclosed the city, each side being twenty-four kilometres long. The wall was bounded by a deep ditch, the earth from which had been used to make the bricks for the ramparts. There were a hundred gateways into the city, each with double doors made of bronze. These were probably faced with enamelled tiles decorated with arabesque mosaics, coloured blue, black, yellow and white.

Within the outer wall was a second, not so tall but imposing nevertheless; then one entered the city itself, where the wide streets crossed each other at right angles. Through the middle of the city ran the Euphrates, which was enclosed between masonry quays which guided its course; at the end of each of the streets which ran down to the river was another bronze gateway, so that although a wide and handsome bridge built on several arches crossed the river to join the two halves of the city together, they could still be closed off to form two fortresses bounded by their respective quays.

On one bank of the river was the royal palace with all its wonders, especially the famous hanging gardens which the Greeks spoke so much of; on the other was the huge mass of the temple of Baal. It was constructed as a series of towers set one on top of the other, with a base two hundred metres square, surrounded by a wall four hundred metres square. It was climbed by external steps. At the top was a sanctuary, containing nothing but a luxurious bed and a golden table. No one ever slept there, except, so it was said, the woman chosen by the gods. The offertories, altars, golden statues and idols of all kinds were placed in the lower parts of the building.

It seems there were houses of more than one storey. This must have been, indeed was, unusual, since the Greek commentators remark on it. The houses had subterranean rooms ventilated by means of those tall narrow shafts which the Persians call "badgyrs" or "wind-catchers", and which enabled Babylonians to spend the hot season in a comparatively cool environment, even if humid and rather unhealthy. All the same, Asiatics still use this method today. There were many large open rooms, decorated with painted bas-reliefs.

Such was the great Babylon when Cyrus, having completed his campaign in Lydia, turned on it. One of its allies was totally destroyed; the other, Amasis, the Egyptian, gave no sign of existence. Nabonidus must have felt defeated from the start, and nothing makes defeat more certain.

Cyrus and his hosts came down from the mountains. They had already entered Assyrian territory and were about to make the crossing of the Gyndes, the river which flows into the Tigris from the east, near the spot where Baghdad stands today, when one of their white horses, regarded as sacred animals, leapt ahead into the water to swim across, being full of youth and strength.

A reconstruction, based on archaeological research, of the temples and palaces in the centre of Babylon.

But the water was rough and throwing up clouds of spray where the waves beat against huge rocks, which hid treacherous chasms; the foal lost its footing and, staring terrifiedly, was swiftly carried out of sight of the appalled soldiers. Unable to help, they were obliged to watch their beloved beast submerge and disappear.

Like the whole army, the king was overcome with sorrow and anger. He swore to punish the guilty river and to humiliate it in such a way that it would never again drown anyone, and that even women would be able to cross without danger. So leaving Babylon to its apprehensions and calculations of escape, he spent the whole summer making cuttings and canals so that the waters of the river were spread out into three hundred and sixty ditches, all shallow. When this had been done, the great king set off again on his campaign.

Left, a Persian soldier's equipment: a dagger hangs from the waist, its point protected by a chased scabbard attached to the thigh to secure it on the march. Right, an Assyrian monarch (Museum of Antiquities, Turin).

The conqueror wished to take the city by surprise. He began by dividing his troops into two divisions.

When his preparations were complete, he brought his troops in rapidly, and on a day when the Babylonian population were celebrating a national feast-day, the Iranians sailed up the Euphrates, scaled the quay walls, broke down the gates on the side streets and took the city almost without a blow being struck, before most of the inhabitants, engrossed with their own pleasures, realised what was happening.

Although Babylon had been taken it was not looted or burned. Cyrus did not destroy the walls or remove the gates. We are not told what became of the king.

The taking of Babylon gave the Iranians an unexpected and quite rare opportunity to demonstrate the liberality of their regime. Amongst the disparate elements making up the population of the defeated state, there was one which had once been a nation taken into slavery but which had gradually, as time went by, found a way of living amongst their erstwhile masters which enabled them to preserve their self-respect and sense of identity as a nation. These were the children of Israel.

In 721 B.C., according to accepted chronology, the Samaritan tribes were carried off to the country of Niniveh. In 589 B.C. a similar fate befell the Jews; in front of their father the children of king Sedecias

43

The above bas-relief, of early Babylonian origin, depicts the seige of a city. Opposite, the Achaemenid lion attacking the Babylonian bull, pictured symbolically on a bas-relief at Persepolis.

had their throats cut, and then his own eyes were put out. Since that time the Jews and Samaritans, carefully preserving their hatreds and animosities, had spread far and wide. Their industrious spirit, love of knowledge, indomitable energy and hatred of strangers had served them in good stead, so that they had become powerful, even formidable.

Their common dream was the re-establishment of the kingdom of Judea, but this time a completely pure and orthodox kingdom, free of the corruption which they firmly believed to have been the cause of their downfall.

This ideal had little chance of becoming reality as long as the Babylonian dynasty reigned, the self-avowed enemy of Jerusalem; but as soon as this fell and they realised what kind of man Cyrus was, Jewish aspirations soared and everything seemed suddenly possible.

A Babylonian king's feast, according to an ancient bas-relief in the British Museum. Note the heads "decorating" the branches of the trees. Right, a golden sword of 500 B.C. (Archaeological Museum, Teheran).

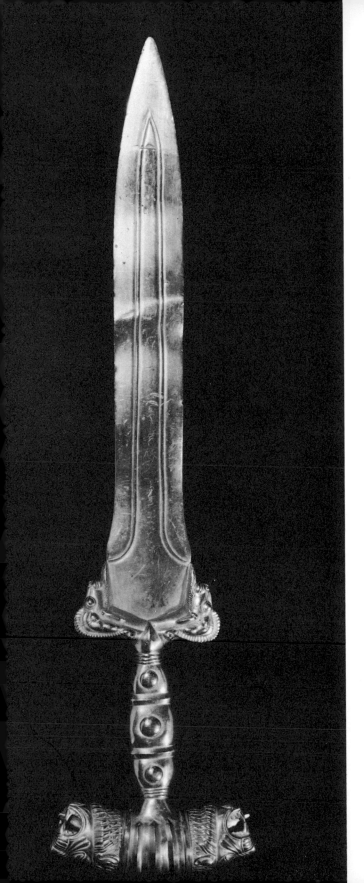

Cyrus did not worship idols. He did not consult oracles; he practised a quite different religion from that of Mesapotamia. Under his regime, which did not differentiate between classes or religions, the Jews were treated in exactly the same way as anyone else; and finally he had overthrown their persecutors. They started to venerate him and offer prayers for an increase in his sway: his weapons belonged to Jehovah. They began to believe that he was an instrument of the true God; it was in any case quite clear that he had been chosen by Eternity to be the master of its armies. Who could deny it? Such was the belief in the Iranian monarch's mission that even the prophets themselves accorded him the title not subsequently allowed to anyone before Emmanuel: that of Christ. They declared that he was the Christ: the "Christ-Cyrus", as may be read in the prophet Isiah.

So, living amongst his old enemies Cyrus found a dignified nation which not only submitted to his power but welcomed him with fervour, respect and the devotion due to the holy instrument of God's vengeance. The Iranian monarch listened kindly to the pleas and supplications with such sympathy that soon after taking possession of his new territories he put forth an edict which permitted the exiles to return to their own country and rebuild their towns. One of their princes, Zorobabel, was placed in charge of the expedition.

The actual text of Cyrus's edict has been

47

recorded by Esdras, and may be paraphrased as follows:

"So speaks Cyrus, King of Persia: Jehovah, God of Heaven, gave me all the kingdoms of this earth, and has Himself commanded me to build for Him a mansion in Jerusalem, which is in Judea.

"Who amongst your people wish to perform this task? May God go with them, and may they go to Jerusalem, which is in Judea, and may they there rebuild Jehovah's mansion.

"And may those others who cannot go, wherever they might live, assist with money, gold and beasts, those who wish to be present with the Elohim who reside in Jerusalem".

Cyrus did not limit himself to authorising the renaissance of Israel. He published a second decree ordering the reconstruction of the Temple, setting forth the dimensions so that it should be fit for the traditional ceremonies, and the materials of construction. The royal treasury paid the cost.

A fragment of Susianian pottery.

Bas-relief (a fish god?) from the ruins of Cyrus's palace at Pasagardes. Remains of the fire temple in the same city.

After consolidating his control of the empire of the Medes and conquering Lydia, then Chaldea and its illustrious capital Babylon, Cyrus set out to submit all the peoples living to the East of his States, as far as India, the area of present-day Afghanistan and Turkestan. Within twenty years he thus built an empire stretching from the Mediterranean to India. He was to perish during an expedition into the steppes near the Aral Sea. We are assured that his antagonist had his head cut off and then plunged it into a cup filled with blood saying: "You thirsted for blood; here you are." His remains were brought back to his capital, Pasagardes, and placed in a monument erected in the middle of his palace gardens.

Cyrus was succeeded by his eldest son Cambyses, who was a drunkard and had no scruples against putting to death his brother, his sister and a multitude of officials. He none the less wished to extend the empire still further and, setting on Egypt, defeated it, then turned his attentions of Ethiopia, which he also conquered in part. Having got himself recognised as Pharoah at Memphis, he adopted the Pharoahs' dress.

Meanwhile an usurper was having himself proclaimed king of Persia. And it was while returning to fight him that Cambyses died from a thigh wound. Darius, a member of the royal family, took on the elimination of the pretender. He himself was to conquer part of India but he was above all to carry out the pacification and organisation of the immense country he ruled, being rightly called the Great King.

The Bible often confuses the Elamites (or descendants of Elam, one of the sons of Shem) with the Persians. It is true that the country of Elam was to come under Cyrus. The very old bas-relief above, which used to decorate one of the Elamite sanctuaries in Susa, depicts a goddess, Ishtar, a man-bull, and a personalization of a sacred palmtree.

3 - The empire of Darius. Persepolis.

The word "khshaeta", or "shah" in modern Persian, was the title of the great barons as well as the king himself. In their own domains the barons were in fact treated as sovereigns in their own right.

They wore gilded buskins just like the Great King; tambourines were played before them as they walked, and their personal standards, embroiderd with their coats of arms, flew wherever they were. Their subjects obeyed only their orders. They lived in great sculpted, ornamented palaces surrounded by innumerable lodges housing their retinue of servants, workmen, dancers, musicians and all the others who made up their court. They also possessed castles in places considered necessary for defence, mostly against the Scythians, but sometimes against the king as well.

Below the shahs, or great barons, came the lords, known as "ratous", or "rad" in present-day speech. These were the sons, relatives or allies of the shahs, and were themselves considerable landowners in their own right. As they were closely connected to the baron in one way or another, or descended from good family, they constituted the first rank of the nobility, and as such their duty was to lead the troops. So it is amongst this class that we find the "acpa-paitis", the "spehbed", or leaders of cavalry, who until the end of the empire were not only military chiefs but also provincial governors and even ministers of state. There are many instances of men of this class being used by the Great Kings to oppose the threat from too-powerful barons.

Under Cyrus, however, all this changed. His successive conquests had given him Media, Lydia, the whole of Asia Minor as far as Judea and the Egyptian border. He had been equally successful in the east and north-east. Apart from the lands given in fief to his military leaders, all the provinces of former Iran were his.

Until then, every feudal baron ruled his own province without regard to any law other than that pertaining to its own people, and which the central government could not change. The rights of the barons, lords and people were upheld by local custom; the Great King could not touch them, and once obligatory military service had been rendered and voluntary contributions for special occasions given him his powers met an unbreachable barrier. All that differentiated the king from the other chiefs was in effect a kind of presidential status and more extensive domains.

This form of political organization, more like a confederation than an empire, had to give way to unification. Darius divided his states into twenty governments. He destroyed neither the fiefs nor local sovereignties; it would have been dangerous for him

A reconstitution of a palace in Persepolis. Left, the Apadana, or great reception hall, with, in the background, the palaces of Darius and Xerxes.

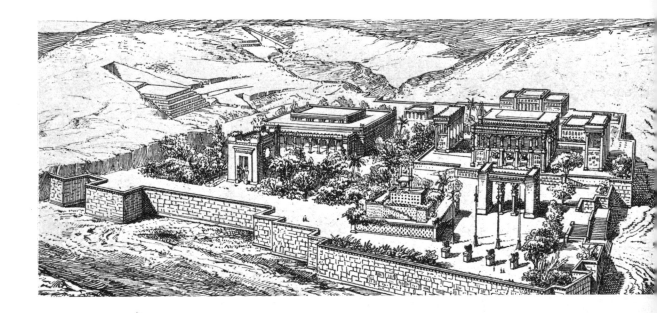

Persepolis, founded by Cambyses, was developed by Darius. The Persians called the town Istakhar, and it was the Greeks who imposed the name of Persepolis—or metropolis of Persia—which has remained famous throughout the centuries. Its situation in a large plain copiously watered, defended by a ring of mountains, was extremely well chosen. It was built on both sides of a stream, the Sirvend, but the royal palaces were built at a distance, almost on the mountain-side, with a view over the whole plain. Their terraces dominated the latter from a height of twenty feet and the stairway up to them was composed of one hundred and eleven steps; it was fifty feet wide so that ten horsemen could climb it in line abreast.

Two masses dominate the ruins of the city: they are remains of the palaces of Darius and of his son Xerxes. The main hall of the first was fifty feet long and decorated with slender columns in height thirteen times their width. The palace of Xerxes was in the same style, but more spacious.

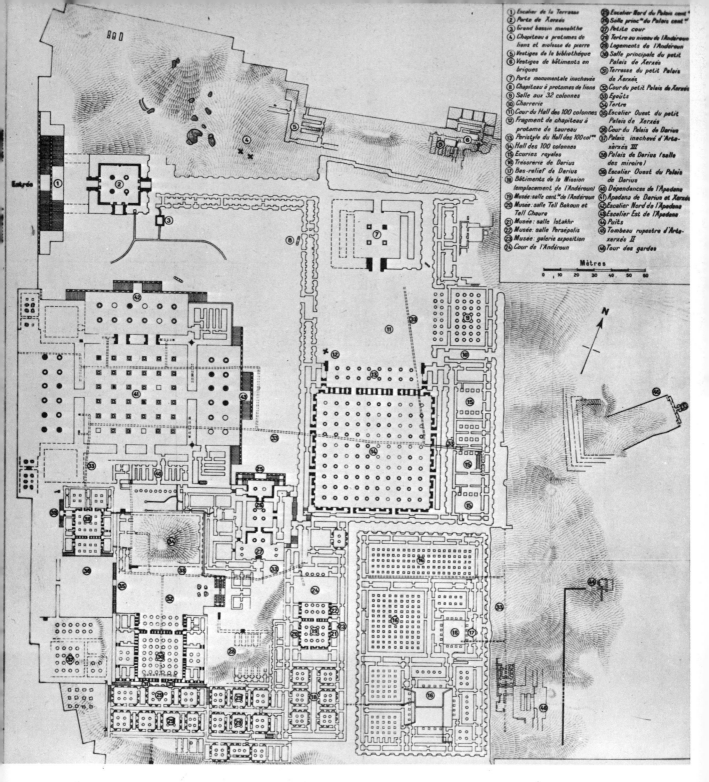

Left, plan of Persepolis at the height of its splendour. Above and opposite, the ruins of the hall of the "hundred columns" and plan of Darius's palace.

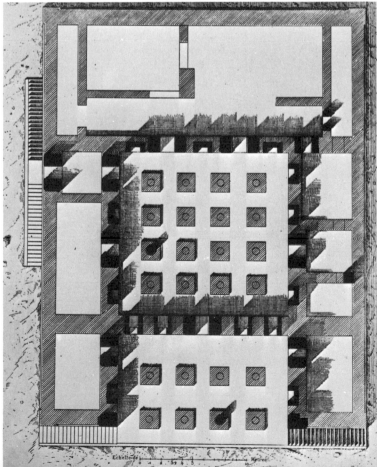

58

Persepolis. The main gate of Darius's palace, together with the hall called the "Hall of Mirrors".

Persepolis. Remains of the Gate of Xerxes. Right, a reconstruction of the entrance to Darius's palace, and the entrance to the Persepolis Museum built with the original materials and set out as in Darius's time.

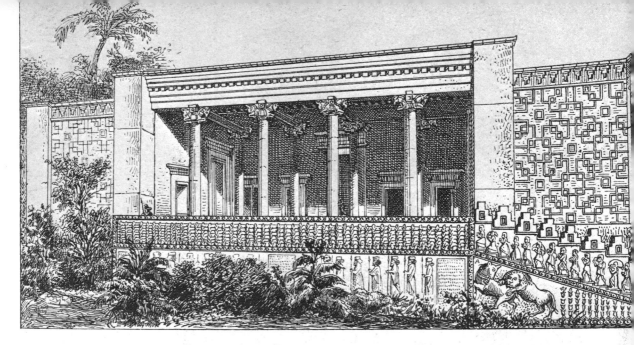

Persepolis. A lion-head capital. An Achaemenid lion-head (detail from the bas-relief shown on page 45, which used to ornament a staircase in Darius's palace). Right, Darius overcoming a lion.

Persepolis. Viewed from the bottom, the impressive palace terrace. Blocks of stone at one of its corners. The approach steps.

to attempt to do so, and in any case he would have undoubtedly failed. He allowed the different nationalities under his sway to retain their own laws, but succeeded in uniting them administratively, a considerable achievement. His officers were the Satraps.

Herodotus refers to the fact that certain nations were not subject to the regime; Persis for instance had no obligations except a contribution it could decide for itself. This privilege dated back to the time when it was a personal fief of Cyrus; when it passed into the domain of the Great King it continued to be treated as in the past, in other words as having only a personal link with the empire. The Ethiopians used to give the king two bushels of god, two hundred ebony boles and twenty elephant's teeth, along with five young native slaves, every three years. The tribes living on the southern slopes of the Caucasus required only to make a gift of a hundred young men and a similar number of girls every five years. Finally, certain Arabs in the Peninsula made an annual offering of one thousand talents' weight of incense.

Herodotus reports that when the tributes were received, the Great King melted down the gold and silver in separate earthenware jars. Ingots were made and placed in the Treasury, and whenever money was needed these were used to make coins which were placed in circulation. So the royal tribute was not intended to be spent; it merely constituted a kind of reserve.

Among the peoples subordinate to Persia, there were many of only moderate or little importance; they each had their own language, customs, system of law, and religion. Darius's genius is shown by the fact that while he established his domination over so many small and diverse nations he never tried to assimilate their populations into Persia but on the contrary respected their individuality. He merely ensured that in every country there was a strong military arm, established in secure fortresses, and placed each region under the control of persons he could trust: these were the Satraps.

They were in fact vice-roys, and nearly always members of the royal family. Just like the Great King, the Satrap lived in a sumptuous palace. He had a personal guard, and the right over life and death; imposed taxes and dispensed justice to the highest level. His only superior was the Great King. However, a representative of the latter, whose duty was dealing with reports and correspondence, was attached to his retinue. The Satrap was obliged to give an account, by express couriers, of everything that happened in his territory. The central authority was represented by the inspectors of Satraps, who always moved about under military escort.

Bearers of offerings to the Great King, decorating one of the staircases in Persepolis.

At the same time, the sovereign maintained a very large court; numerous wives, a harem, eunuchs, functionaries and innumerable guards; his guests were counted in thousands every day; he maintained endless numbers of horses, chariots, carriages; extensive property, palaces, gardens, parks, in every part of the empire, which were constantly being rebuilt and replanted at his orders; his expenditure on rare and costly objects, decoration and luxuries of every description was enormous, and was obliged to be in order to conform to his people's conception of the magnificence appropriate to a monarch.

The numerous and varied peoples subject to the Great King were obliged to send him valuable tribute each year. Only the Persians were exempt. Darius fixed the amount of gold and silver or natural produce (corn, horses, cattle, rare woods, cloth, incense, etc.) which each owed him. Some nations had to supply him numbers of young men and girls.

68

Bearers of tributes to the Great King (east staircase of the Apadana). In following pages, servants bringing dishes or presenting animals (west staircase of Xerxes' palace and right side of the terrace of Darius's palace).

An Armenian tribute brings jewels to the Great King; an Indian arrives to offer a mule; others present cloth (east staircase of the Apadana and the palace of Xerxes).

The royal seal. Darius (called Darajaoucha) on his throne. (Hall of the Treasury at Persepolis).

The expense of maintaining the army must also be remembered. The fitting out of the cavalry, the upkeep of the garrisons, the manufacture and maintenance of vehicles and chariots, was an expense charged to the provinces.

Also there were public works, such as castles, bridges, aqueducts, drains, canals and reservoirs. Although in some cases these were paid for by the Treasury, in general the cost was met by the countries which benefited from them, and the same applied to the roads.

Darius is attributed with the instituting of a mail service. However, I consider that just as the road system dates back before Persian domination to Assyrian times, so I believe the mails to pre-date the prince's reign. Even so he may well have re-organized a service which must have been severely tested by the wars of Cyrus, the conquest and subsequent upheavals. Perhaps he can also be credited with extending it to the whole empire, as an essential part of his vice-roys' functions, as it had not previously existed in the western provinces. Be that as it may, this is how the mails operated. At each station, an official kept horses constantly at the ready. When a courier arrived from the preceding station, the man mounted one of his fresh horses and set off immediately, and rode with full speed to the next station with the dispatches, irrespective of rain, snow, heat or darkness; on arrival he handed over the mail to another rider. By

A golden ornament belonging to Darius (Archaeological Museum, Teheran). On an immense rock several hundred feet high, rising above the road connecting Babylon with Ecbatana, Darius caused a lengthy inscription to be carved recording all his great deeds.

At the end came the following declaration: "Whoever you are, read this inscription and know that everything written in it is true and that I have achieved many other things which are not recorded here". (Picture opposite).

Below, detail from bas-relief. Men from conquered countries support the throne of the Great King.

this method news arrived at its destination as rapidly as it ever did in Europe before the railways were built. Perhaps this was the most powerful means of authority at the disposal of the Great King; it was central to the unity of the empire so far as the word had any meaning in those days.

While carrying out his reforms, the Great King befriended a movement which was to overshadow everything else. He was not its creator, but he supported and propagated it. I am referring to the religious reform to which Zoroaster gave his name, and to which Darius bears a similar relationship as that of Constantine to Christianity in a later epoch. The Zoroastrian revolution is one of the landmarks in the history of humanity.

Darius established the empire. What he built lasted not only to the end of the dynasty of the Achaemenidae; the principles still hold to this day. Alexander only enlarged the empire; he did not change it.

Below and in succeeding pages, capital and bas-relief in Persepolis.

A race-course near Susa (land of Elam). Tributes driving a chariot.

King Darius struck gold and silver coins, called darics. Although thick and irregular in shape they were of practically pure metal and were used in particular for paying the troops. The coins shown opposite belong to a later period, but are identical for all intents and purposes.

4 - Religion. The priesthood. Susa the capital.

Most evidence seems to show that Zoroaster was by birth a Mede. The name means simply "golden star". It was natural that Darius should be attracted to a system of ideas born along with his own dynasty, and one which seemed to meet the needs of the times. The king wished to try and reconcile the interests of the Iranians with those of the Semites, and naturally supported a philosophy likely to bring this about.

To begin with, Zoroaster overthrew the old idea of geography, whereby the pure world consisted only of the sixteen countries originally inhabited by the Iranian race, and all other places came under the influence of evil spirits. Such a theory was clearly not appropriate to an empire which stretched from the Ionian sea all the way to Africa.

For the old division, Zoroaster substituted another. He declared that the earth was divided into seven regions, all equally pure and deserving of veneration.

Zoroaster and his disciples thus wished to change the system of beliefs held by the Iranians until that time, and any imperial subjects who adopted the new faith were to be brothers, irrespective of where they were born. This had something of the appeal of Christianity for the Gentiles much later, with its promise of including them in a new Israel, no matter how far away they were.

The reformer's greatest innovation was to organize the spiritual world. Ormuzd or Aboura-Mazda, personifying the divine idea, became the leader of the amshaspands, "amesha-çpentas", or immortal saints, the actual spirits of the pure parts of the universe. Van-Humano or Bahman was the thought which lit up intelligence; Asha-Vahista or Ardi-Behescht was purity, the antagonist of evil; Khshatra-Vairya or Shahryver was water, the vehicle of life; Çpenta-Armaiti, the earth, universal provider; Haurvatat, wealth—not the sort which Plutus personified for the Greeks and Romans, but rather the abundance resulting from agricultural work, always ennobling for those who undertook it. In their present-day dialect the Parsees call this amshaspand Khourdad. The last of these great gods who did not share creation but animated each of its principal forces, was Ameretat, who gave immortality to the whole, or rather he was himself the immortality of the whole; he was defined as constituting the joy in the heart of every being faithful to him. The celestial army, everywhere spread out under the eyes of the believer, was not to be denied. There were "yazatas" or "izeds", the spirits of all individual things in nature, which were conceived of as having a corresponding pure representation in heaven. Nations, countries, peoples all had their izeds.

The days also had their izeds which inspired them to produce good; a herd of horses had

its ized, as long as it contained young and healthy animals; in short, the ized everywhere represented healthy mental and physical life, correlating to a celestial body whose actions controlled the earthly part of the being or thing, and maintained the universal bond existing throughout Ormuzd's creation.

What might be called the ideal substance of the world extended even further, going beyond individuality. As well as amshaspands and izeds there were the ferouers or fraourvas, the perfect types, so to speak, of all created beings without exception, provided that they were pure and belonged to life: ferouers of the men and women of Iran, ferouers of dogs, horses and cattle; ferouers of everything in existence. These types, created by the active forces in nature, were worshipped in their pristine state in cases where they had never since shown themselves; but they were accorded the same veneration when they appeared in material form, and later when they had abandoned that form. One cannot help remarking how profound this doctrine was and how it contrasts with teachings of eternal punishment and reward.

Another important institution was that of the clergy. The effect of this was felt even in the heart of Persian Islam, where there was flagrant imitation of Babylonian customs.

Amongst the Medes there was a, tribe which bore the name of Magi. Herodotus tells us this, but he makes no reference to

A Mede leading a lion cub and an Assyrian tribute. (Museum of Art, Cleveland, and Persepolis).

A Fire temple, at Nak-e-Rostem. Right, part of the decoration of the Gate of Xerxes, at Persepolis.

Symbol of royalty
(the Lesser Palace
of Xerxes) and a
royal lion-head.
(Archaeological
Museum, Teheran).

any connexion between them and the Iranian priesthood. The word "maga", meaning "great", might have been adopted by the tribe and the religious masters without the latter being aware of the little political unit's existence. From the information we possess it appears that the Magi priesthood was formed very early on, concerned with both dogma and worship, and during the whole Achaemenidan dynasty slowly perfected its beliefs and gave its theology breadth and cohesion. Its main preoccupation was the sort of authority over the minds of the faithful which the old religion did not achieve; the concentration of spiritual power

had become indispensable for the spread of the philosophy of which the priesthood was arbiter. The amount of ceremonial, and obligations, had been multiplied; morality was subject to stricter rules; sins and omissions, now more clearly defined, required elaborate expiation which could only be carried out with the assistance of priests; supernatural intervention in human affairs demanded skilled interpretation by someone trained in the magical art; for all these reasons the priest became a far more important figure than he had ever been before.

Cyrus and Cambyses had no capital city as such, no more than Charlemagne, and for

the same reason. Both were constantly at the head of their armies, the former establishing the northern and western frontiers, and the latter conquering the immense, wealthy southern areas; neither had time to establish a fixed base, and as their continually active lives were more concerned with expansion than administration, their empire lacked any kind of centre. Darius, who had the task of co-ordinating all they had achieved, placed his seat of government in the city of Susa, in Susiana. A *Chronicle of Susiana* complacently expatiates on the country's resources. It assures us that everything one could desire in the way of food for man and beast is there in abundance, at the cheapest price possible. Wheat, barley, rice, in fact every cereal, grew there to perfection. The light, wellwatered soil could be easily ploughed with a donkey, and if horses were used this was only to finish the job quicker. Oranges, lemons, limes, figs, pomegranates, and every conceivable kind of fruit grew in profusion. The salt had a very special flavour. A straight-stemmed reed grew there which provided writers the world over with their very best paper. Their melons, marrows, cucumbers and water-melons were truly exquisite. Cotton grew there like nowhere else. It is surprising that the author, in his enthusiasm, made no reference to the sugar-cane, which

had once been grown extensively in Susiana, but which had not been cultivated for a few centuries. He says that at one time the whole country was given over to cultivation. Everywhere were gardens of ease, orchards and fully-burdened fields. Running out of sight on every side were glistening canals carrying fresh water to the furthest reaches.

This enchanting picture of Susiana is no doubt accurate as far as it goes, but omits the other side of the coin. Being in love with his country, the writer makes no mention of its disadvantages; they would spoil the picture. His country, so admirable in other respects, was also the home of malignant fevers and endemic diseases induced by the extreme heat of the climate and the vapours of its extensive marshes.

Poisonous snakes and harmful insects abound there now, and in my opinion have always done so. All sorts of reptiles glide in and out of the houses; scorpions, huge venomous spiders, whose bite can often be fatal, mosquitoes of all sizes, torment the inhabitants and prevent this otherwise fortunate country from becoming an earthly paradise.

Strictly speaking the people of Susiana were not Iranian. They derived from a mixture of negroes, or Asian Ethiopians, and Semites, who had interbred over a long period.

Susa was founded a long time before the reign of Darius, who only, like his successors,

94

extended an already major city which had been the capital of the powerful Elamites. The author of the Chronicle of Shouster states that the city dates back to very early times and contained the very first human habitations. Men at first lived in caves and holes in the ground, exposed to the weather and attacks from wild animals. Housheng taught them to build houses of dried earth, wood and reeds, to place them near each other and surround them with walls and ditches; Susa was the first city to be built in this way.

According to the same author the name means "The Beautiful". He says it is an old name, and the city had the shape of a falcon with outstretched wings, the symbol of sovereignty. While the foundations of the houses were being built, Housheng, who was watching the workmen, saw a dog emerging from the workings; it trotted off and returned a little later carrying a bone which it took behind one of the walls and proceeded to gnaw. Housheng was very struck by this and took it as a bad omen. But one of his friends, a wise and learned man, explained that it meant that the people would be obliged to go out and seek their necessities,

and even go into foreign parts to find what they needed. This prophecy was indeed applicable to a nation of cultivators and traders.

Susa was not fortified; but it had an acropolis built on a hill in the south-west of the city, on the banks of the river. North of this extended the grandiose palace of the Great Kings. The city itself was set on the east, covering an area sometimes estimated as a hundred and twenty stadia in circumference, or sometimes much less, depending on the period in which the particular writer lived. As in the entire Tigris valley and the greater part of Persia, building materials consisted of kiln-fired or sun-dried bricks cemented with natural pitch.

Statue discovered at Susa

The palace was magnificent, surpassing those of Ectabana and Persepolis. The book of Esther describes it as surrounded with woods and gardens, and when referring to the feasts given by king Ahasuerus, speaks of "white, green, and blue hangings, fastened with cords of fine linen and purple to silver rings and pillars of marble: beds of gold and silver, upon a pavement of red, and blue, and white, and black marble".

.. and inscribed bricks also from Susa.

*Remains of ancient Susa: detail of a frieze
from a palace and a sarcophagus.*

The famous "Valley of Tombs" of the Achaemenid sovereigns; from left to right, hypogea
(note the cruciform facades) of Artaxerxes I,
Xerxes, Darius I, Darius II. Between the first
two, the Fire temple shown on page 88. Right,
a close-up view of the tomb of the Great Darius.

From left to right, façades of the tombs of Xerxes, Darius II, Artaxerxes I,
Above, the tomb of Artaxerxes III.

No sovereign in the world had ever been as powerful as the king of Persia, no one had ever possessed such wealth. Usually he wore a long, full, purple robe with gold motifs. On his head a crown set with precious stones. Golden rings through his ears, necklaces and bracelets at his nect and wrists. At all times, incense was burnt before him. He could not be approached without permission, under pain of death, and everyone introduced into his presence, even the highest in the land, had to touch their forehead to the ground. Outside his gardens, he never moved on foot.

These door-posts at Persepolis show the Great King followed by a servant waving a fly-whisk and, another carrying a parasol.

Designs on the north
door of the Hall of
a Hundred Columns;
they depict the ten
thousand "Immor-
tals", as the Great
King's personal guard
were called.

5 - Xerxes. His wife. The story of Esther.

It was in the reign of Xerxes, the son of Darius, that there began to appear for the first time, and in an unmistakable manner, the consequences of the weaknesses inherent in the organization of the empire. Although they moved in gilded air, sparkling with riches, strong and powerful, they were to finish up scrabbling in the mud; the first signs of the dreadful collapse were not long in showing themselves, even though final ruin was not to come for some time yet. Cyrus had the glory of founding the monarchy; Darius consolidated it with admirable authority; but nothing can prevail against natural law, and from the time of Xerxes the slow descent began.

The Orientals call Xerxes Artaxerxes or Ardeshyr: the difference is not important, since "arta" is merely a prefix meaning "great". They also give him the name Bahman. The use of variable titles and surnames is of great antiquity in Asia, and the same person may be described in many different styles. So there is nothing strange in finding Darius's successor variously called Bahman, "Vohumano", Xerxes and Artaxerxes.

The Persians also gave him the surname Dyraz-Dest, or "Long Hand", on account of the extent of his conquests.

After his great campaigns and his return to Iran, Xerxes fell in love with his daughter Homai, surnamed Scheherazade, and married her, which reduced his son Sasan to despair. The young prince, who was disinherited in favour of the queen, left the court and went to live with the baron of Nishapur, whose daughter he married. He died not long after, leaving his descendants in possession of a pastoral country, where for centuries they reigned over nothing but shepherds and sheep spread out over mountains and plains.

It is clear from this incident that as Homai was able to disinherit the legitimate heir she must have been able to exert considerable influence over the Great King. This is a direct reflection of the power of the harem, a power which did not exist in Cyrus's time. It started to make itself felt under Cambyses, when his mother and sisters started to intervene in matters of state. It developed further under Darius as a result of the natural authority pertaining to such women as Atossa and Artystona, Cyrus's daughters, regarded even by their husband as more direct representatives of regal power than himself; Parmys, another of his wives and the daughter of Smerdis and granddaughter of Cyrus, also possessed great influence, as did a fourth, the daughter of Otanes, whose dowry was the pledged allegiance of the great barons. From this time onwards the court became accustomed to the presence of as many political parties as there were queens, not to mention the various cabals formed around the king's favourites.

After Darius, in Xerxes' reign, the influence of the harem became even more marked. The style has been set; many people came to depend on the good offices of the women; the eunuchs exercised power through them; it was no longer possible to change the organization of the court, and domestic intrigue flourished more and more.

When the sovereign had been on the throne for three years and felt secure against his rivals, he ordered a convocation of his lords and servants, in other words his barons and high state officials, in order to impress them with the reality of his power. This great assembly would last for one hundred and eighty days, or six months.

This is one of the finest examples of the old Iranian constitution. Neither Cambyses' violent temperament nor Darius's centralizing genius could destroy the essential principles of a liberal régime; even Xerxes, we see, felt bound to bring a parliament together for six months in which he would hear pleas, discuss problems and settle contentious matters, as well as put forward his own proposals for general approval.

At the end of the six months, when all the business had been completed, the Great King gave a farewell feast lasting seven days. Everyone was invited, not only the lords and officials, but the whole population of Susa, from the highest to the lowest.

The feast took place in the royal park.

A bas-relief shows a noble (actual height 1.70 metres) in the presence of Darius. Note the censer between the visitor and the sovereign.

Enormous marquees protected the guests from the heat of the sun; the ropes holding them up passed through ivory rings fastened to marble columns. Pavements of beautifully inlaid mosaics had been laid down, and innumerable paintings decorated the splendid scene.

The feast was worthy of such a setting. Food was served on golden dishes, and wine in unlimited quantities was poured from amphorae made of the same precious metal.

King Xerxes wished this seven-day feast to be an occasion of joy and happiness, where everyone could come and go as they pleased and eat and drink to their fill. All that mattered was that good order should be maintained.

While the nobles and populace were enjoying themselves, the queen for her part was entertaining the women in the gardens and showing them natural splendours the equal of any feasting. The queen's name was Vashti, so the Bible tells us; we can recognize the Zend word "Vahisti" in this, meaning "the excellent, holy one".

On the seventh day, just before the official end of the feast, Xerxes ordered the seven eunuchs in charge of the harem to go and find the queen, so that he could place her crown on her head before all the people and show them her amazing beauty. But she refused to present herself in public as the king wished, which greatly upset him.

This was a conflict between Iranian and Semitic customs. In Iranian tradition there

The reconstructions seen here have all been based on the most detailed historical and archaelogical research. Hall of the Hundred Columns, Apadana.

was no objection to women being seen out of doors, and the two sexes ate together at table; this followed from one of the oldest principles of the race, which gave great respect to wives and the mothers of soldiers. Semitic ideas were quite different; they considered women as merely love-objects, and therefore to be kept hidden on the assumption that any man who saw them would immediately desire them; also, what was secret and mysterious was somehow more worthy of respect. Not to show oneself at all, or only rarely, was the stamp of nobility. When Xerxes ordered the queen to appear before his people he was thinking in the style of the Iranian aristocracy. The queen took the attitude natural to the customs of Susa and the pride of her rank.

The slight the king had received in front of all his subjects from his wife's behaviour was made a very serious affair. If he had been the absolute monarch some people suppose, nothing would have been easier than for him to arrest his wife and have her executed on the spot. But he did not do that. He put the case before his judges, who according to history were always with the king and without whom the state could not functions; they had achieved this elevated position on account of their knowledge of the laws and institutions of their ancestors.

Judgement was given. It was held that as the queen's disobedience in such important circumstances reflected not only on the king's prestige but also on all his subjects,

Bearer of a precious vase.   Dancers, on a fragment of pottery. (Louvre, Paris.)

irrespective of their rank, and brought into doubt the whole matter of marital rights, there should be brought into effect a law, to be incorporated into the constitution of the Medes and Persians, forbidding the queen ever to appear in public with the king and for her functions in this regard to be transferred to another woman; in this way all wives throughout the empire would be reminded of their status in marriage.

The king agreed to this edict, but it did not mean that the queen was totally repudiated, merely that she could never appear with the king in public and that her place would be given to another woman. It was indeed a severe punishment; but it was considered necessary so that every woman would understand the consequences which followed disobedience to one's husband. But the king retained the option, as did every aggrieved husband, of ceasing the punishment when he considered it fit; this is what happened with Vashti, and after a little while she resumed her full rank and presence.

But before this happened the king embarked on a series of love affairs whose fickleness only seemed to demonstrate the power which his estranged wife held over his heart. From all over the empire the most beautiful girls were brought to tempt his palate. As soon as they arrived they were taken into one of the interior palaces and placed in the care of the eunuchs, who were trained to bring them to the height of their attractiveness. For six months they were massaged with rare

Head of a prince and a sovereign's seal (Teheran Museum).

oils and myrrh to bring their skin to perfection; for another six months they were smoothed with perfumes and delicate cosmetics, and given special food. When the experts in these matters considered the moment was right the girl was informed that the moment had come for her to go to her imperial lover. Whatever she desired in the way of clothes or personal ardornment was immediately granted her. It was wisely understood that in her wish to please she might be inspired to ideas which would not have occurred even to those versed in such arts.

On the following morning, the girl would be taken to another palace under the charge of the eunuch Sahasgaz, who was in control of the concubines, and would not go to the king again unless she was expressly ordered.

Amongst the girls so presented to the king was a Jewess whose own name was Hadassa, "myrtle", but had been given the name Esther, "the star", on entering the harem. She was an orphan and had been brought up by her uncle Mordecai, who was so impressed by her beauty that as soon as

A eunuch, on a Babylonian bas-relief.

he heard that girls were being recruited for the king put her forward as a candidate. She turned out to be very much to the king's taste, and as she had taken the trouble to be kind and polite to the eunuchs in charge of her she was their favourite as well.

Mordecai led the kind of life which is still quite common in Asian cities. He used to leave his house in the morning, go to the palace, and spend hours sitting in the shade with the people he knew there, exchanging news and getting deviously involved in palace intrigue.

He counted on Esther's good offices to improve his situation, and had impressed on her not to tell anyone who she was or where she came from.

One day, Mordecai was lucky enough to overhear from some people idling at the palace gate news of a plot being hatched by two of the eunuch door-keepers, Bigthan and Teres, who where planning to seize the king and kill him. No doubt they were hoping to replace him with one of his brothers. Mordecai told Esther what he had heard, and she passed it on to the king. Investigations were made; the report was confirmed and the two eunuchs hanged. In accordance with his practice the king recorded in his journal what had happened; then, pre-occupied with other matters, dismissed it from his mind.

However, the prime minister, who was greatly in the king's favour, was at that time a man called Haman, the son of Hammedatha. The king liked him and he was consequently a very powerful man. When he used to arrive at the palace in the morning, surrounded by his servants and followers, he used to notice that Mordecai failed to rise to show his respects along with the others. Although all sorts of comments were made about his behaviour, the Jew continued with his impertinence, and in the end Haman became incensed with it. Silent and angry, he pretended to disdain the offender; but when he learnt he was a Jew he resolved to revenge himself on the whole of his race, the old enemy.

Having been prevailed upon by the Jews' religious leaders, Cyrus had authorised the rebuilding of the temple of Jerusalem. He had issued laws to this effect; but the hostile presence of Assyrian colonies in Palestine and the reluctance of the children of Israel themselves to leave their comfortable establishments in a wealthy country to enjoy the rather sterile joys of life in their ancient homeland cooled the leaders' ardour and detracted from the court's good intentions. The Persian kings were usually well-disposed towards the Jews, whom they saw as a natural counter-weight against other Semitic peoples, especially the Assyrians; but when they came to have Semites as ministers there were new discussions about the rebuilding of the temple, and those who advocated it were made out to be subversive and disaffec-ed elements. Haman added credence to this debate through his quarrel with Mordecai, and on the promise of a thousand talents of

122

silver to be paid into the treasury was given authority by the king to dispose of the affair in any way he thought fit. He was given the royal seals by Xerxes, who assured him that his actions would receive the full backing of the law.

As soon as he received the authority Haman issued an edict to all the provincial satraps, city governors, and feudal chiefs ordering them that on a certain date they were to arrest all Jews and put them to death. The spoils were to belong to the executioners, a sure way of encouraging zeal. The general massacre was fixed for the 13th of Adar, the twelfth month.

When they heard of this plan, the terrified

From his palace in Susa, not far from magic Chaldea, king Darius could look out over the rich plain and nearby mountains. His grandson was to build another palace (with a throne-room 7,000 metres square !). Two enamelled friezes from the latter have been recovered and are now in the Louvre: the frieze of the Archers, composed of men of the royal guard, two details from which are seen here, and the frieze of the Lions (detail on the next page).

The frieze of the Lions is composed of nine lions, all alike, each of considerable size: 3 ½ metres long. Below, part of the frieze of the Archers before restoration.

Jews fell into despair. Many of them gave public display of their horror by covering themselves in sackcloth and ashes. One of these was Mordecai, who lay in front of the palace so garbed but did not enter the court as he had been used to, as he was not allowed to appear there so dressed. Esther had been warned of what was going to happen and was terrified; she sent for Hatash, one of the royal eunuchs placed in charge of her, and asked him for advice as to what to do.

Mordecai felt she should use her influence with the king. Esther was not in favour. She pointed out that no one was allowed to appear before the sovereign unless expressly summoned, and that to infringe this ruling was to risk one's life; in any case her influence was not very great, as it was more than a month since Xerxes had sent for her. This shows clearly, taken with the fact that the king always made her come to him and that he never visited her in her own apartments, that the beautiful Esther had neither the rank nor standing of a wife.

Mordecai disapproved of his niece's caution. He told the eunuch to try and make her understand that it was not only a question of the Jewish nation but that she herself was in danger; she would die along with all her co-religionists, living in the palace as she did, the enemies of her race would not spare her. How did she know that her special position had not been granted her by God in order to deliver her people? If this were so, how could she dare to ignore the respon-sibility placed on her?

Esther finally gave way to his pleading, mixed with threats, and told him that in spite of the prohibitions of the law and her extreme terror, she would do what he wished and speak to the king; she would first of all fast for three days and nights, neither eating or drinking, and required the whole Jewish community to do the same, in order to predispose the Almighty in her favour. Mordecai promised they would, and went away with hope restored.

At the end of the three days, when Esther considered she had sufficiently fasted and prayed, she prepared herself to show her most attractive appearance, then left her apartments and presented herself in the great hall before the throne in which the king was sitting. She was trembling from the audacity of her action; but at the same time she also probably looked charming, for Xerxes, instead of displaying anger at such an infraction of a rule imposed to spare him from the tumultuous importunities of harem intrigue, turned his golden sceptre towards her, to show she was forgiven.

She touched the end of it, and the king, feeling amorously disposed and forgetting he had not seen for a month asked her, "What do you wish, queen Esther, and what have you come to ask for? If it is half my empire, you shall have it".

Esther confined herself to asking the king to dine with her that same day together with Haman, which was granted. This was a

signal favour which was well worth the trouble she had gone to. It is understandable that she should attach such store to it that she asked the king to repeat the favour the following day, to which Xerxes agreed.

For his part, Haman was not less delighted than the Jewish concubine. He felt he had been honoured by this woman whose beauty so pleased the king; he had been admitted into the company of the two lovers, and there has never been a court, whether in the time of Xerxes or Louis XIV, when it was not considered a tremendous advantage for a favourite to be be invited in such circumstances. So he fully appreciated his good fortune. He boasted about it to his wife Zeres and his friends, whom he specially brought together in order to tell them about his triumph; but he added bitterly, "I am rich, I have beautiful children, the king has raised me above everyone, and now queen Esther has invited me to her meals with her master, yet I still cannot overlook Mordecai's insolence".

At this, Zeres and his friends replied, "Build a gallows fifty cubits high and hang Mordecai from it, then you can enjoy your dinner with Esther."

Lamp-holder and gold bracelet (Louvre and University Museum, Philadelphia).

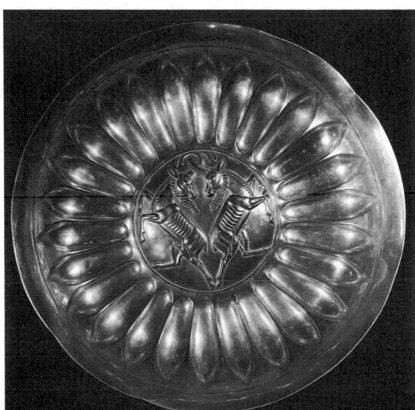

Gold dish from Xerxes' period (Levy Collection, Geneva).

Silver pitcher (Art Museum, Cincinnati). Gold handle of a whetstone. (Teheran Archaeological Museum). Silver ibex set with gold (Louvre, Paris). These pieces date from the time of Darius and Xerxes.

132

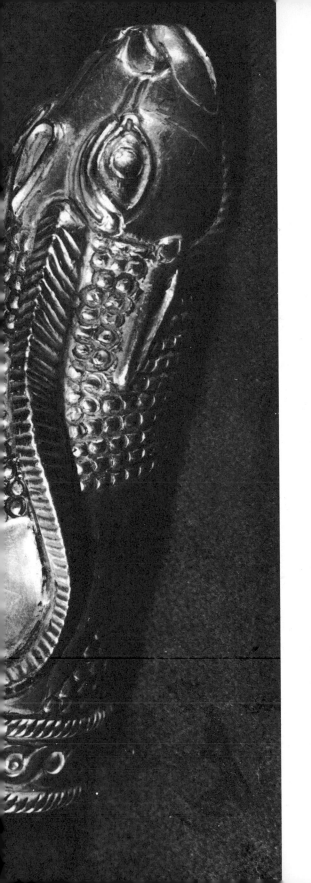

133

Haman was easily persuaded, and gave orders to prepare for the execution of the man who had defied him. However, despite the arbitrary powers Asiatic officials are commonly supposed to have possessed, it was not an easy matter for Xerxes' favourite to hang a man. Haman was determined on it, but it was only a stubborn idea; he began to hesitate; it was only because he was driven by anger, encouraged by his friends and intoxicated with his latest honours that he contemplated building a gallows for a miserable Jew. We may judge from this that in the empire no one could freely take the life of any subject, and if any violence of this sort was planned it was a dangerous procedure for even the highest placed.

While the minister was indulging in anger, an event occurred which he could hardly have foreseen. The king had difficulty in sleeping the night before and had begun to read the journal in which he recorded the events of his reign.

The passage he chanced on was the account of the conspiracy between Bigthan and Teres, when Mordecai had played so useful a role. The king interrupted his reading to ask what reward Mordecai had received. "Nothing", he was told.

This information appalled the king, who thereupon asked if any of his ministers were waiting outside. Precisely at that moment Haman entered intending to ask the king to issue a decree ordering Mordecai's death.

We can see from this that he had given the matter some thought and had decided that he could not take on himself the responsibility for the Jew's execution. In the Greek and Roman republics there was no such compunction.

The king gave Haman no time to explain what had brought him there; he immediately asked him his opinion on the best way to honour someone who deserved particular distinction. The favourite thought the king was referring to him, and did not spare himself; he said that the hero should be dressed in the royal robes, the holy crown placed on his head, mounted on the sovereign's own horse, and led through the main streets of Susa by all the great nobles on foot, who were to cry out in a loud voice, "Here is the king's favourite!"

Xerxes thought these were suitable proposals and immediately ordered Haman to find Mordecai and tell him what he had just said. He did this, and when he returned home, red with anger, and told his wife what had happened, she became very concerned and remarked that if Mordecai was indeed a Jew, which she had not realized, the plan which Haman had concocted against his nation could not succeed and might well end in disaster for its author. But there was no time to discuss the matter, for at that moment the king's servants arrived to conduct Haman to the queen's dinner party.

The meal was well advanced when the

Stone vase, 400 B.C.
(Levy Collection, Geneva.)

Capital from the palace of
Artaxerxes in Susa (Louvre,
Paris).

king, who was in good spirits because of
the wine and Esther's attentions, asked her
to tell him what it was she really wanted
from him, assuring her that nothing would
be refused. Esther no longer hesitated; she
begged him not to have her put to death, nor
the people from she had sprung.

Quite astonished by such an unexpected
plea, Xerxes asked her what she meant and
what enemy threatened her and her nation.
She pointed to Haman, and Xerxes, who
would not dream of exterminating a section
of his subjects, not knowing how to reply
and believing he was becoming embroiled in
one of those palace intrigues the kings
feared, suddenly got up from the table and
went out into the garden.

When he saw the king's indecision, Haman
lost his head. Instead of following his master,
he stayed behind and threw himself on
Esther's couch, passing imploring hands over
her. The king returned and saw this; his
wrath exploded; he thought, or pretended to
think, that his minister was insulting the
queen, and expressed himself with such
violence that the servants threw themselves
on Haman and covered his mouth to prevent
him speaking. One of the eunuchs, named
Harbona, cried out, "He even has a gallows
ready to hang the very Mordecai who saved
the king's life!"

This was the final stroke; at a gesture from
the king, Haman was dragged to the gallows
and hanged.

So Esther and her uncle and all their race

triumphed. Haman's possessions were confiscated and given to Esther. Mordecai took Haman's place and received his seals of office. Henceforward he presented a very repectable figure, dressed in a white robe and purple cloak, with a golden crown on his head. Throughout the empire Haman's fellow-conspirators were sought out; many hundreds were put to death, including the former minister's ten sons.

The king himself was not happy about this slaughter. He had tried to calm Esther, but she had his word, and the Bible informs us that she caused no less than seventy-five thousand to be put to death.

This representation of an equestrian combat decorates Xerxes' tomb.

6 - Culture. Writing.

Like their Scandinavian and German cousins, the Iranians have never been gifted artistically. Neither under the Achaemenids, the Arsacid dynasty, or later the Sasananians, or even in Moslem times, did Persia possess its indigenous style; but it did transform borrowed styles, Assyrian, Indian, Greek, or Roman, into its own characteristic form. This is what gives it its originality. Even the Greeks did not invent their own style; their basic conceptions came from the Assyrians, and they only developed them gradually into a form which the original authors had not been able to achieve.

Dress was brilliantly coloured, both in peace and war, as is clear from surviving cameos and medals.

Hair styles varied greatly. The second Arsacid, Tiridates, wore his hair short and curled in the Greek fashion. On some coins the secondary princes are shown with their hair dressed in our fifteenth century style covering the ears. This lasted some time, and Pacorus is depicted like this. But at the same time, and even before Pacorus we see far more elaborate hair styles and curly beards; sometimes there would be no beard, but a well-developed moustache. With the Volagases, Indian hair styles were introduced: very complicated and built up high, with curls and tresses; the beard was curled in rings.

Tunics seem to have been made of silk, or perhaps of wool embroidered in all sorts of colours, with gold and silver thread running through. Lace was much used for collars, cuffs and hems. Necklaces and bracelets in profusion were indispensable. Rare furs were in demand and very costly. Boots were of tooled leather.

An example of hair-style (Persepolis).

Horse being led by a tribute.

Women's dress was no less magnificent and highly-coloured than the men's. Portraits show that their hair styles varied greatly, and they spent as much time adorning their hair as the men, which is only to be expected. Coins show the head of queen Musa piled up with a veritable edifice of hair; nothing could be more elegant, or complicated. Other princesses are shown on coins with equally complicated coiffures. We can well believe that these Asiatic styles were highly popular, since they were imitated even in Rome, where emperors' wives prided themselves on looking like Parthian ladies. But fashion could change, and towards Trajan's time they used to make statues with changeable hair-pieces so that they could keep up with the times. One portrait shows a queen with her hair smoothed quite flat and parted into three large plaited tresses set with ribbons ending in bows, surmounted by a diadem.

The columns of the Apadana in the setting sun.

Designs at the base of columns, in Persepolis. The second is 2 metres in diameter and 1.15 metres high. Right, remains of the Hall of the Hundred Columns.

*Spirals on capitals
and designs from
a column base, in
Persepolis.*

These inscriptions were on the walls of Darius's palaces (left) and on Xerxes'. Examples of cuneiform writing.

The writing of the Persians, like that of the Medes and Assyrians, was of the king which has been given the name cuneiform, made up of two elements, the wedge and the nail, and written from left to right. Generally speaking, cuneiform writing appears to be made up of nailshaped marks, whose size, angle, width and combinations correspond to specific meanings. Inscriptions were engraved on special tablets, as in Persepolis, on stone slabs, sometimes even on rocks, or painted on pottery.

"The role of the Persians in the history of civilisation appears both trivial and awe-inspiring. This people had an instant of complete, dazzling life. Hardly had they emerged from the deserts of Central Asia, still barbarians, with no literature, no art, no scientific knowledge, than they saw themselves as the owners and masters of the civilised world. For two centuries they took possession of, and condensed the supreme results of, the efforts of mankind over five or six thousand years. — All that the human soul had dreamed of, all that the intellect had produced, all that the imagination had brought forth since the beginning of the world, was seized on by this newly arrived race which knew how to enjoy it with an ease and a noble calm which was not lacking grandeur... By breaking down the resistance of twenty different nations by submitting to the same yoke so many disparate races, it sapped, so to speak, the last remaining energies of the ancient East and prepared a gigantic and easy prey for the mounting ambition of the Greeks." (Gustave Le Bon.)

Paving-stones from the entrance of the Apadana, and, even more ancient, white paving from the palace of Cyrus, at Pasagardes (right).

149

Objets d'art from the Sasanian period: a harnessed horse, a silver bowl showing a king surrounded by dancers, a ewer of gold. 6th. century A.D. (Selikowid Collections, New York and Walkis Art Gallery, Baltimore).

Note on the Sasanians.

During Antiquity Persia for a time dominated world history, but we must remember that the country came into new importance at the beginning of our own era, under the reign of the Sasanians.

In the meantime the country had been conquered by Alexander, who, with the forces of Macedonia and the alliance with the Greeks, succeeded in overcoming the considerable armies of Darius III. After Alexander's death, Persia was ruled by the Seleucids, for about eighty years, to be followed by the Arsacids, who founded the Parthian empire, which lasted until 229 A.D. At that time, the son of Sasan, Ardeshir, discontented with his lengthy disgrace, revolted and after defeating king Artaban IV became master of Central Asia. But his empire was far from as extensive as the old Persian one; the Romans occupied Syria and Asia Minor, and even areas beyond the Euphrates in certain places.

As he was desirous of restoring Cyrus's empire in full, Ardeshir ordered them to evacuate these regions; in vain. He died in 238, leaving his son Sapor I to profit from the anarchy prevailing in the Roman empire. Sapor defeated Valerian, whom he flayed alive and whose skin was hung as a trophy in the temple. A hundred and fifty years later one of his successors, Balas, was attacked by the

Huns and had to cede part of his kingdom and pay them tribute. But under Cabad the situation was reversed: first victory over the Indians, then the Huns, then the Greeks. Cabad died in 531, and his third son, Chosroes, who succeeded him, was to reign over a territory almost as vast as that of Darius, stretching from the Mediterranean to the Indus and from the Caucasus to Arabia and the Egyptian border. A hundred years later, it is true, following the death of Mahomet, the Persians were to fight against the Arabs, and be completely destroyed after a ferocious battle lasting three days. The Moslems crossed the Euphrates and caliph Omar received the Persian crown. Chosroes attempted some kind of resistance in the mountains, with the help of the Tartars and even the emperor of China, but was finally assassinated. Under the Sasanians Persia became not only an extremely powerful country again; it was also noted for its art and culture, to which numerous museum pieces bear witness.

Index

153

Depósito legal B. 31967-71   Printer, industria gráfica sa
Tuset, 19   Barcelona   San Vicente dels Horts   1971

Printed in Spain